PEOPLE
WHO MADE
A DIFFERENCE

NELSON MANDELA

D0171101

Titles in the
PEOPLE WHO MADE A DIFFERENCE
series include

Louis Braille
Marie Curie
Father Damien
Mahatma Gandhi
Bob Geldof
Mikhail Gorbachev
Martin Luther King, Jr.
Abraham Lincoln
Nelson Mandela
Ralph Nader
Florence Nightingale
Louis Pasteur
Albert Schweitzer
Mother Teresa
Sojourner Truth
Desmond Tutu
Lech Walesa
Raoul Wallenberg

North American edition first published in 1992 by
Gareth Stevens Children's Books
1555 North RiverCenter Drive, Suite 201
Milwaukee, Wisconsin 53212, USA

This edition copyright © 1992 by Gareth Stevens, Inc.;
abridged from *Nelson Mandela: Strength and spirit of a free
South Africa*, copyright © 1990 by Exley Publications Ltd.
and written by Benjamin Pogrund. Additional end matter
copyright © 1992 by Gareth Stevens, Inc.

Library of Congress Cataloging-in-Publication Data

Pogrund, Benjamin.
 Nelson Mandela : speaking out for freedom in South Africa /
[abridged by] Jamie Daniel, Benjamin Pogrund.
  p. cm. — (People who made a difference)
 Includes index.
 Summary: Presents the life and career of the long-imprisoned
leader of the African National Congress.
 ISBN 0-8368-0621-2
 1. Mandela, Nelson, 1918- —Juvenile literature. 2. Civil rights
workers—South Africa—Biography—Juvenile literature.
3. African National Congress—Biography—Juvenile literature.
4. Anti-apartheid movements—South Africa—Biography—
Juvenile literature. 5. Political prisoners—South Africa—
Biography—Juvenile literature. 6. South Africa—Biography—
Juvenile literature. [1. Mandela, Nelson, 1918- . 2. Civil rights
workers—South Africa. 3. Blacks—Biography.] I. Daniel, Jamie.
II. Title. III. Series.
DT1949.M35P65   1992
323'.092—dc20   [B]   91-50541

**For a free color catalog describing
Gareth Stevens' list of high-quality
children's books, call**

 **1-800-341-3569 (USA) or
 1-800-461-9120 (Canada)**

PICTURE CREDITS
Associated Press 27, 51 (lower), 58, 59;
Mary Evans Picture Library 9; Gamma
Liaison 12; International Defence and
Aid Fund for Southern Africa 4 (both), 7,
11, 15, 18, 20 (both), 21 — Ben
Maclennan 10, Eli Weinberg 24 (both),
25, 28, 39, 40 (upper), 45, 46 (lower), 52,
Jurgen Schadelberg 31, 33, 36, 38, Dave
Hartman 53, 57 (both); Ali Kumalo 48,
49; Magnum — Eve Arnold 16, Ian Berry
19 (both), Abbas 34, 35, G. Mendel 54-55;
Peter Magubane 23, 40 (lower), 50-51;
Pictures by Tony Nutley from the TVS
film *Mandela* 43 (both); Tom Redman
cover illustration; Spectrum Colour
Library 46 (upper).

Series conceived by Helen Exley
Editors: Amy Bauman, Patricia Lantier-Sampon
Editorial assistant: Diane Laska

Printed in MEXICO

1 2 3 4 5 6 7 8 9 96 95 94 93 92

PEOPLE
WHO MADE
A DIFFERENCE

*Speaking
out for
freedom in
South Africa*

NELSON
MANDELA

Jamie
Daniel

Benjamin
Pogrund

Gareth Stevens Children's Books
MILWAUKEE

Above: After twenty-seven years in prison, Nelson Mandela was released on February 11, 1990. Here Mandela is shown with his wife, Winnie, surrounded by supporters.

Right: In London, Nelson and Winnie Mandela greet a cheering crowd with the salute of the African National Congress (ANC).

Freedom

At 4:17 p.m. on February 11, 1990, Nelson Mandela walked through the gates of South Africa's Victor Verster Prison. Hundreds of journalists waited for him outside. Their television cameras made it possible for over one billion people around the world to see Mandela raise his hand in a clenched-fist salute as he left prison for the first time in twenty-seven years.

While most of these people had heard Mandela's name, few had any idea of what he looked or sounded like. The cameras showed a tall black man with white hair and a lined face. In spite of his seventy-one years, Mandela walked with grace and confidence. This first impression of great strength was confirmed when he addressed the world at a news conference in the Cape Town city hall two hours later. His voice was firm as he began, "I greet you all in the name of peace, democracy, and freedom for all."

Nelson Mandela had been offered his freedom several times, but he had always rejected it in the name of his cause — the freedom of his fellow black South Africans

"I have dedicated my life to this struggle of the African people. I have fought against white domination, and I have fought against black domination. I have cherished the ideal of a democratic and free society in which all persons live together in harmony and with equal opportunities. It is an ideal which I hope to live for and to achieve. But if needs be, it is an ideal for which I am prepared to die."
Nelson Mandela in his statement at the Rivonia trial, October 1963

5

and the destruction of the racist policy known as apartheid.

Apartheid

Apartheid is a policy of extreme discrimination based on a person's skin color. The policy was invented and is still practiced by white South Africans. The word *apartheid*, which is pronounced "apart-hate," means "separateness" in Afrikaans, the language spoken by the white South Africans called Afrikaners. Apartheid first became known to the rest of the world in 1948. In that year, the Afrikaners gained control of the government and began to implement tougher racial segregation policies.

Permanent settlement

The policy of apartheid had begun in South Africa long before 1948, however. The ancestors of today's Afrikaners were seventeenth-century Dutchmen who established a stopping point for their trading ships at Cape Town in 1652.

The stopping point grew into a permanent settlement. The settlers began farming and came into conflict with the native Khoikhoi people, who roamed across the land to graze their cattle and sheep. The Khoikhoi, who had previously been on friendly terms with the settlers, resented the loss of their grazing land. Soon there were armed conflicts between

the two groups. Because the Khoikhoi had only bows and arrows, they were no match for the settlers' guns. Hundreds of Khoikhoi were hunted down and killed.

Within a few years of the establishment of Cape Town, the pattern for future race relations in South Africa was established. White settlers believed they were superior to the darker-skinned native peoples and used them as slaves. The situation grew more complicated when some European whites and native peoples mixed, creating a large group with a mixed racial heritage who became known as "Coloured."

The Afrikaner Nationalist government took power after winning an election in 1948 in which only whites were allowed to vote. The first cabinet, shown here, established the policy of apartheid under which nonwhite South Africans have suffered ever since.

Dislike of authority

In 1795, Britain took control of the cape,

and British settlers came to live there. Now English-speaking Europeans lived alongside Dutch farmers, who were known as Boers. The Boers found it difficult to deal with the new British authorities, since the Boers had always been in charge before.

When Britain abolished slavery in 1833, the Boers left. They moved away from the cape in 1835 and began what they called the Great Trek into the African interior. There they established the independent states of Transvaal and the Orange Free State, where they spoke their own language of Afrikaans and isolated themselves from the rest of the world. They continued to use black native peoples as servants and workers. A third Boer state, Natal, fell under British rule in 1843.

The greatest warriors

Through the early 1800s, southern Africa was in turmoil as black tribes fought against each other for power and land. The first black people met by white settlers were the Xhosa people, who lived in the east. In the interior, there were also the Sotho, the Pedi, and the Swazi. The greatest warrior tribe was the Zulu, who lived along the east coast in what is now Natal. Their king, Shaka, led his people to many victories in battles between the tribes.

Eventually the settlers became involved in the tribal wars. They usually won in

Even the fierce Zulu warriors couldn't defeat the guns of the British army. The Zulu were defeated in 1879 in the Battle of Ulundi. British soldiers burned many villages after the battle, as this drawing from that time shows.

battles against the tribes because of their more sophisticated weapons. By 1879, when British troops finally defeated the great Zulu army, many native people had lost their cattle and had been forced off their land.

For many years, South Africans had lived primarily by farming. But this changed because of two important discoveries that pushed the nation toward industrialization. The first was a giant diamond found by a farmer in 1866. People rushed in from all over the world to prospect for diamonds. They exploited natives as laborers in the diamond mines.

"City of Gold"

A second important discovery was made twenty years later in 1886: gold. People again rushed in from all over the world to seek their fortunes. A city developed in the midst of the gold rush, called eGoli, Zulu for "City of Gold." The white settlers named the new city Johannesburg.

Systems of control

The diamond fields were controlled by the British under colonial rule, but the gold mines were in the heart of Boer-controlled South Africa. The Boers guarded their isolated areas and were horrified by the numbers of Europeans who came into their country in search of wealth. The Boers did not want foreigners to vote or have a say in their government.

Native people were made to work the mines, remaining in poverty while white mine owners grew wealthy. As the mining industry grew, more workers were needed. Black men had to leave their tribal homes in the country to come work in the poorest of conditions in the mines.

Rules were drawn up to keep the families of these black workers from joining them. One rule enforced segregated housing. White workers lived comfortably in new towns with their families, while black workers were made to live away from the towns in poor areas without water supplies or sewer systems.

Above: After diamonds were discovered in South Africa, thousands of people flocked to the mines. White workers were given skilled jobs, while black workers were given the unskilled jobs that paid much less.

Opposite: Johannesburg was not a "city of gold" for everyone. Many black workers had to live in compounds like this, where living conditions were poor. The apartheid laws didn't allow these workers to bring their wives and children with them.

11

Black males worked for as long as they were needed, and then they had to return home. Because of this complicated system of laws and regulations, blacks lost control over their own lives.

The Boer War

Tensions rose between the British and the Boers, and in 1899 the Boer War broke out. Within months, British troops had captured the cities of Johannesburg and Pretoria in the Boer state of Transvaal.

The Boers refused to surrender. Britain brought in another 250,000 troops to fight. They also put Boer women, children, and

old people in concentration camps as part of a harsh policy to force the Boers to give up. A peace treaty was finally signed in 1902. But the Boers never forgot the humiliation they suffered both during the war and immediately afterward.

Eventually, Britain tried to consolidate both white groups — the Boer-Afrikaners and the English-speakers. The Union of South Africa was established as a part of the British Commonwealth on May 31, 1910. Black people made up the great majority of the population within this union, but they still had only second-class status. They were not allowed to vote and were treated as aliens in their own country.

Other nonwhite groups suffered as well. The mixed-race Coloured people were discriminated against, as were the many Asians who had been brought to South Africa by the British to work in the sugarcane fields. They weren't even allowed to travel to other parts of the country without first getting special permission from the government.

Birth of the African National Congress

Naturally, black people felt their lower status was unfair. They formed an organization in 1912 called the South African Native National Congress, which was later renamed the African National Congress, or ANC, for short. The ANC requested that black people have a voice in the government. It also requested Britain's protection against the white government, but Britain refused. After that, the South African government enacted even stricter laws against the black majority. One such law made it illegal for black miners to work at skilled mining jobs that would have paid them higher wages. Blacks were also forced to leave their lands and homes to live in "native reserves," special areas away from the towns. Their farmland was then simply given to whites.

More segregation laws

Because some blacks worked in the towns, new laws set up segregated black "townships" there. Black workers lived in the townships while work lasted. After that, they were expelled from the townships and sent back to the reserves.

The most effective means of controlling the movement of black families were the pass laws. Black people had to carry special identification papers listing where they were allowed to travel. If a black person was caught without proper papers, he or she was arrested and sent to prison. More than ten million people were arrested and imprisoned under the pass laws.

Such laws gave the white government almost unlimited power over South Africa's black people. Any black person

or group could be ordered to move at any time or be forced to stay in any one place. The rules restricting black people grew tougher and increasingly unfair.

Nelson Mandela is born

Nelson Rolihlahla Mandela was born into this situation on July 18, 1918. According to custom, he was given a European name, Nelson, as well as a name in Xhosa, the language of his Tembu tribe. That name, Rolihlahla, means "stirring up trouble."

Nelson's father, Henry Gadla Mandela, was a chief of the Tembu tribe. Chief Mandela had enough wealth to own a

The African National Congress was formed in 1912 to secure rights for South Africa's blacks. For almost fifty years, the African tribal nations under the leadership of the ANC would use nonviolent resistance in their struggle for a fair deal. Violence wasn't used until 1961.

horse and cattle and to support four wives and twelve children. Nelson and his three sisters were the children of Nosekeni, also called Fanny, the chief's third wife.

Nelson Mandela's village, Qunu, was located in the Transkei reserve. Qunu was a quiet place — the only way to get there was to take dirt roads. There Nelson and his family lived in three separate huts called rondavels. One hut was for sleeping, another was for cooking, and the third was used for storing food. Nearby was the family's field and the pasture where the cattle and goats grazed. Looking after the animals was Nelson's job.

Rolling hills cover the Transkei, the region where Nelson Mandela was born. The land is beautiful, but it has been damaged by over-grazing and erosion because it must support too many people.

Nelson's mother could not read or write. Because she wanted Nelson to learn these things, she sent him to the local school to be educated. There he was remembered as a quiet boy who worked hard.

Chief Mandela died when Nelson was ten years old. A relative, Chief Jongintaba, took care of Nelson after this as if he were his own son. This was the custom — relatives in Xhosa families looked after each other, sharing food and shelter whenever it was needed.

The Great Place

In 1928, Nelson moved with Chief Jongintaba to the Great Place, the royal living quarters at Mqekezweni. There he shared a hut with his cousin, Justice.

Every day after school, Nelson and Justice looked after the cattle in the fields. In the evening, they brought the cows back home to be milked. Then they would sit around the fire and listen to the elders tell stories about "the good old days, before the coming of the white man." They heard about their ancestors' brave deeds in the days when they were free.

A feast

A great feast was prepared when Nelson finished primary school. But this was not the end of his education. Jongintaba then sent him to a top high school for black pupils and later to college at Fort Hare.

"Almost every African household in South Africa knows about the [1921] massacre of our people . . . when detachments of the army and police, armed with artillery, machine guns and rifles, opened fire on unarmed Africans, killing 163 persons . . . simply because they refused to move from a piece of land on which they lived."
Nelson Mandela, speaking in Ethiopia in February 1962

Opposite, above: A worker displays a gold brick. Until very recently, the black workers who mined this gold had little share in the wealth it created. Opposite, below: Poverty is widespread among the black population of South Africa. However, most of the white population live very well.

Below: At nineteen, Nelson Mandela was a grown man. After his father's death, Nelson was cared for by Chief Jongintaba, a relative in his father's family.

Because the educational system was as segregated as the rest of South African life, there were separate schools for the different racial groups. Most of the money was spent on white schools, while many black children had no opportunity to go to school at all. There were few who had as much education as Nelson Mandela.

At his high school, Mandela lived in a dormitory with the other boys. The dormitory was plain, and the boys were served simple meals. Breakfast and supper were the same — hot water with sugar and a piece of bread. Lunch was hot corn porridge, and sometimes there was a little meat. Only on Saturdays were the boys allowed to walk to the nearest village, where those who could afford it bought a meal of fish and chips.

In 1938, Nelson Mandela finished his secondary schooling. He had done so well that Chief Jongintaba decided he should go on to the university at Fort Hare. The university was also segregated, but its students included Coloured and Asian South Africans as well as blacks.

Suspended from the university

Living conditions at Fort Hare were generally better than they had been at the high school. But the food was still very poor. Although the students complained about it, nothing was done. The students organized a strike to protest the bad food, a strike in which Nelson Mandela took part. Because of this, he was suspended.

Chief Jongintaba told Nelson to apologize to the authorities and return to school. Instead, Nelson and Justice ran away to Johannesburg. To get money, they took and sold two of Chief Jongintaba's oxen. The chief was so angry that he tracked the young men to the city and ordered them to return home. Justice agreed to go back, but Nelson asked to stay in Johannesburg to study law. Chief Jongintaba agreed.

Johannesburg

Mandela was not used to life in a big city. Although Johannesburg was not more than fifty years old, it was South Africa's largest city. Mandela found it both exciting and confusing. In the northern part of the city were the comfortable homes of the city's white residents. Black residents lived in townships like Sophiatown and Alexandra, where they could still own land, although these areas were crowded, poor, and plagued by crime.

Nelson Mandela was twenty-three years old when he arrived in Johannesburg in 1941. South Africa had sided with Britain in World War II, and because of the war, there was a lot of work in industry. Workers streamed into the townships from the rural reserves to work in the factories. For black South Africans, this was an exciting time.

When Mandela arrived in Johannesburg, he lived in a poor township that had no electricity or running water. It was at this time that he decided to join the ANC and dedicate his life to helping his people struggle for equality.

There was talk of a democracy after the war. Black people looked to the future with hope. The ANC became popular again. Its new president, Dr. Alfred B. Xuma, was a doctor who changed the ANC into a modern political movement.

Marriage for Mandela

Nelson Mandela liked the excitement of the city. He lived in the township of Alexandra, surviving on very little money. He continued his studies for a bachelor of arts degree and then studied law.

It was also during this time in Johannesburg that he met Walter Sisulu. They became close friends. Sisulu had a great influence on Mandela's life. Although they couldn't know it then, they would both soon become important leaders in the struggle for black South African freedom.

Mandela met Sisulu's cousin, Evelyn Mase, who was a nurse. They fell in love and were married in 1944. The couple had little money and couldn't afford either a wedding feast or a place to live. Evelyn's sister generously offered the couple one of the small rooms in her home. In typical African family generosity, no one expected them to pay for this hospitality.

Family life

After a while, Nelson and Evelyn Mandela were able to have a house of their own in

During the 1960s, several African countries won independence from colonial rule, and wearing traditional African clothing became popular. In this picture, Nelson Mandela wears traditional clothing.

Orlando. Now they were able to help support other members of their family. In spite of the crowded conditions, everyone managed to find a space in the small house, even after the birth of the Mandelas' son, Thembi. Nelson and Evelyn had another son, Makgatho, and two daughters named Makaziwe. The first daughter died when she was still a baby, so the second was given the same name.

Nelson Mandela loved his family but he was kept busy away from home. Evelyn worked as a nurse to support the family while Nelson continued his law studies at the University of Witwatersrand, where most of the students were white. Only a few black students were allowed to attend this university, and they had to be exceptional. But blacks still had second-class status on campus and were allowed only to study. They could not take part in any sports or social events.

Mandela studied law so that he would be able to work later as a lawyer for his people. But it was hard for him to study while living in the poor conditions of the township. Like most other black families living in tight quarters, the Mandelas had to manage in their small home without hot water or a modern toilet.

Travel was also a problem for people in the townships. Mandela traveled to the university by bus, but he had to wait for the special buses marked for "nonwhites."

African nationalists

Walter Sisulu also introduced Nelson Mandela to the African National Congress. Soon Mandela was working with a group of young men who wanted the organization to take radical action. In 1943, they formed the ANC Youth League, which pushed for change within the ANC. The group wanted to promote African nationalism, the idea that black African culture was as important as white culture. The members believed that any important change would come about only through confrontation with the whites.

They also argued for non-collaboration, the idea that blacks should refuse to take part in segregated activities within the

To survive, many township families are forced to share a single dwelling with their relatives. The Dabula family, seen here at mealtime, consists of twenty-five people who share a four-room house. Only two people in the entire family have jobs.

government. They felt that since black people had no real power in the government, they shouldn't support the illusion that they did. Some African nationalists went so far as to suggest that blacks should refuse to cooperate with any other racial group, including the other oppressed racial and political groups.

Mandela in opposition

But Nelson Mandela didn't feel this way. Despite the university's restrictions on socializing, he met with white and Asian friends whom the Youth League also opposed. He made lasting friendships with some of these people. And he loved debating politics with them. He had a gift

Once the policy of apartheid was officially established in 1948, signs like these became common. Left: In the 1950s, a Johannesburg streetcar stop is marked for use by "Native" or black passengers. Right: After 1948, signs such as these were seen in railroad stations across the country. They became illegal only in 1990.

for combining his fine mind and his personal warmth — qualities that made him a natural leader.

By 1947, Nelson Mandela was elected general secretary of the Youth League. But in 1948, the Afrikaner National party took power. This group won because of its support for a policy of strict apartheid. The party's aim was summed up in the Afrikaans word *baaskap*, which means "to be the boss."

Racial pigeonholes

The new government carried out its harsh policies through the Population Registration Act, which put everyone into an official racial category. Each black person was "classified" according to his or her tribe.

For years to come — and, in fact, until the Population Registration Act was finally repealed in 1991 — this policy led to all sorts of horrible situations. Sometimes, for example, one member of a family was classified as Coloured while the others were said to be white. Because members of different racial groups could not live together, the family was split apart.

Marriage between people of different groups was also illegal, and the country was divided into a network of segregated areas. Specific groups could live, work, and own businesses only in specific areas. Whites took the best areas for themselves,

Some white people put up signs of their own. This sign's warning is made even more threatening by the use of the word kaffir, *a term used to insult black people.*

and more than 3.5 million nonwhites were forced to leave their homes and land.

In the 1950s, a new plan turned the native reserves into the so-called homelands. All black people not employed in urban areas had to return to the homeland to which they were assigned. These homelands were used to keep blacks who weren't needed as workers away from the cities.

Enforcing apartheid

The apartheid system took a stranglehold on the country. Signs everywhere proclaimed, in Afrikaans and English, "Net blankes — whites only." Every bus and train in the country was segregated. Some jobs were even reserved for white workers only.

Parks in the cities were set aside for whites only, and so were libraries. The beaches were segregated, with the best and safest beaches reserved for the whites. Blacks and other nonwhites were not allowed into concert halls or theaters.

The government decreed separate schools for black children, and education in these schools was clearly inferior to that of the whites. Officials wanted to make sure blacks knew that there would be no way for them to advance.

The government also enacted laws that allowed it to ban organizations as well as people. Over the years, hundreds of people

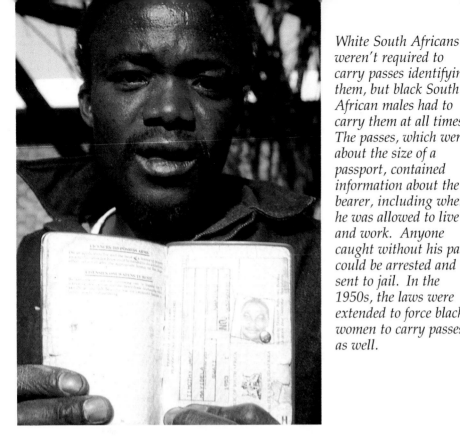

White South Africans weren't required to carry passes identifying them, but black South African males had to carry them at all times. The passes, which were about the size of a passport, contained information about the bearer, including where he was allowed to live and work. Anyone caught without his pass could be arrested and sent to jail. In the 1950s, the laws were extended to force black women to carry passes as well.

would be banned, which meant their personal freedom was severely limited. The laws would soon allow the government to arrest anyone it pleased and to keep people in jail without ever bringing them to trial.

Political tensions increase

As things grew worse, Nelson Mandela played a key role in making the ANC Youth League more prominent. By the end of 1949, the organization convinced the ANC national conference to adopt an outline for a plan that opposed white rule.

"Who will deny that thirty years of my life have been spent knocking in vain, patiently, moderately, and modestly at a closed and barred door? . . . [T]oday we have reached a stage where we have almost no rights at all."
Chief Albert Luthuli, president of the ANC, 1952

27

Mandela did not share all the views of his fellow Youth League members. He believed it was important to work with people of different racial groups and political views. The events of May 1, 1950, convinced him he was right.

On that date, there was a strike to protest the government ban against the Communist party. The Youth League did not want want to support the strike. In the morning, Mandela is said to have urged other blacks to report to work as usual. The strike ended in tragedy when police opened fire and killed eighteen people.

The deaths made many people angry, and there was a day of protest organized

Nelson Mandela was a busy lawyer even while he continued to work in politics. For years, he and Oliver Tambo were partners in a law office. Their clients were usually people who desperately needed help in protecting themselves from the apartheid laws.

on June 26. This time the ANC supported the protest, as did Mandela. In fact, he was the chief organizer. After this, he was willing to see the ANC cooperate more with other groups.

Mandela, the leader

Mandela now rose into the upper ranks of the ANC leadership. He was one of four deputy presidents of the group and was president of the Transvaal branch, which had its headquarters in Johannesburg.

He was also professionally successful. He and Oliver Tambo, another ANC member, started a law practice. There were only a few black lawyers in Johannesburg, and things weren't easy for them. They weren't given equal respect in court. But Mandela and Tambo always had many clients seeking their help.

Even having such an office was an achievement for them, since apartheid didn't allow most blacks to have offices in the city. Once, the government ordered Mandela and Tambo to go back to the all-black area, but they appealed and gained permission to stay where they were.

Challenging the government

But Mandela had less and less time for his legal practice. He was again asked to organize a big ANC protest. The protest, planned for 1951, would be a challenge to the government's racial laws. Blacks and

"Nelson Mandela was jerked out of bed. . . . His house was surrounded by the police. . . . The homes of twenty other Transvaal activists were raided. They were all arrested. This . . . would become commonplace in the years to come."
Fatima Meer, in her book, Higher than Hope: A Biography of Nelson Mandela

"Nelson's day was taken up by the court, so he spent the evenings, and late nights, attending to his legal practice and ANC work. As a result he usually returned home . . . in the new day. . . ."
Fatima Meer, in Higher than Hope: A Biography of Nelson Mandela

other nonwhites were urged to break the laws wherever they could.

More than eight thousand people responded to the challenge. Some sat on park benches marked "whites only." Some entered offices through the "whites only" doors, and a white supporter of the protest was arrested for going into a township without permission. Many, including Mandela, were arrested. He paid bail to be able to continue the struggle. He spoke at hundreds of meetings, urging others to join in the nonviolent protest.

The ANC believed strongly in nonviolence. They were influenced in this by their religious beliefs and also by the lessons of resistance taught by Mahatma Gandhi. Gandhi, an Indian lawyer, had protested against discrimination when he lived for a time in South Africa. Later he used nonviolent protest to free India from British rule. Nonviolence was also a good way to make it less likely for protestors to be shot by the police. But despite the ANC efforts, violence sometimes did erupt.

The protests were called off when the government passed new laws enforcing apartheid even more strictly. For example, someone sitting on a "whites only" bench could be fined, whipped, or put in prison.

Mass police raids

The police made mass raids on homes and offices of protest organizers. They seized

documents and arrested the leaders, including Mandela. At their trial, those arrested were found guilty and sentenced to jail. But the judge knew they had worked to avoid violence, and put them on probation instead of sending them to jail.

Although he was free, Mandela became a target for government harassment. He and other leaders could not attend any meetings, and he was not allowed to leave Johannesburg for six months. But Mandela continued to write speeches that others read for him at meetings.

The police have harassed black South Africans for as long as Nelson Mandela can remember. Here policemen beat demonstrators in a picture taken during the 1970s. Such violence has been common throughout the history of the ANC's struggle.

31

During the 1950s, the ANC continued to be the victim of government harassment. But many South Africans still believed the laws could eventually be changed, and so they continued to support the ANC.

The effects of apartheid were felt by everyone. Jules Browde, a white friend of Nelson Mandela, remembers telling Mandela about something he experienced. He and his wife, who were not racist, were going out for the evening, leaving their young son with a black maid. The boy cried, and said, "I don't want to be left with a black face."

Mandela had experienced a similar situation in his own home. Once, when white visitors had come to visit and left, one of his children asked, "Why do you have white people here?" Mandela replied, "Not all white people have white hearts. Some have black hearts."

Fighting back

It was a troubled time for the ANC. The government's power was increasing. It took control of black education, establishing a new system called Bantu Education. This system was obviously one that made black people inferior.

In response, the ANC called for a boycott of the schools. But many parents didn't want to participate until they were assured that their children would still be educated. Those who did boycott the schools paid a heavy price: their children weren't allowed to come back to school.

Banned

In September 1953, it seemed as if Mandela's political role would come to an end. A new set of banning orders confined him to Johannesburg and demanded that he resign from the ANC and other organizations. He wasn't allowed to attend any gatherings, not even social affairs such as dances or dinner parties.

Mandela refused to recognize the legality of the bans. The ANC also refused, using a new slogan: "We stand by our leaders." This meant that, even if a leader pretended to resign from the ANC, he secretly remained a member. This was risky, since anyone who did not obey the bans could be jailed.

So Mandela continued his work behind the scenes, hiding his activities from the police and their informers. He helped plan a meeting called the Congress of the People, which was held in Johannesburg on June 26, 1955. Thousands attended, and Mandela watched the activities from the cover of a nearby house.

On the second day of the meeting, the police came in and detained everyone. But those present at the meeting were still able to approve the Freedom Charter, a document that set out basic demands for a free South Africa.

In 1952, the South African government declared that Nelson Mandela would not be allowed to leave Johannesburg or attend any meetings. When he did not obey, he was arrested. Here he is seen in court after receiving a suspended sentence of nine months in prison.

Whites and blacks working in South Africa's gold mines have always been treated differently. Above: Black miners, who make up more than 90 percent of the workers, usually live in crowded compounds that allowed only men, thus keeping them apart from their families. White miners can live with their families in pleasant homes. Opposite: An overhead view of a village for white miners.

The Freedom Charter

The ideas in the Freedom Charter came from ideas suggested by people all over South Africa. It clearly outlined the democratic goals of the freedom movement, including the following:

The people shall govern!
All national groups shall have equal rights!
The people shall share in the country's wealth!
The land shall be shared among those who work it!
All shall be equal before the law!
All shall enjoy equal human rights!
There shall be work and security!

The doors of learning and of culture shall
  be opened!
There shall be houses, security and comfort!
There shall be peace and friendship!

The charter concluded with the words, "These freedoms we will fight for, side by side, throughout our lives, until we have won our liberty."

The Freedom Charter was a reasonable document that listed basic rights and hopes. But the government thought it was dangerous. Civil authorities struck back eighteen months later by arresting Mandela on December 5, 1956.

TREASON TRIAL

The
ACCUSED

DECEMBER
1956

Mandela, Walter Sisulu, and Oliver Tambo were among the many people of all colors arrested that day. All were charged with high treason, a very serious crime. Almost all of the leaders of the ANC and its allies were paralyzed by the trial, which would drag on for four and a half years.

Winnie Mandela

In 1956, there was a great change in Nelson Mandela's personal life. His marriage to Evelyn Mase ended as she grew weary of the pressures of his political life. Her husband had no time for his family. His hours were divided between the treason trial, secret activities for the ANC, and his law practice. She and Mandela were divorced in 1957.

Mandela was later introduced to a young social worker named Winifred, or "Winnie," Nomzamo Madikizela. They were married in 1958 but had to obtain special permission to celebrate a traditional ceremony at Winnie's home.

Winnie has said, "I knew when I married him that I married the struggle, the liberation of my people." She knew she would have to share her husband with the many people with whom he worked or who came to him for help.

The ANC splits

Meanwhile, there were more problems

Opposite: In mass police raids carried out in December of 1956, 156 people from all groups were arrested and charged with trying to overthrow the government. The long, drawn-out trial that followed, known as the Treason Trial, lasted more than four years. Nelson Mandela, now a leader in the ANC, was among those accused. Here he can be seen with the others, in the middle of the third row from the bottom.

Nelson Mandela married Winnie Nomzamo Madikizela, a social worker living in Johannesburg, on June 14, 1958.

for the ANC, including a serious split within its ranks. While Mandela now accepted the idea of cooperation between the races, it still alarmed some of his African nationalist colleagues. They argued that the ANC didn't oppose apartheid strongly enough, and that it had given up on its original goals.

It was hard to counter these charges, since the ANC leadership was in a state of confusion because of the many bannings and trials. Its finances were in a mess, too. In 1959, this situation led a group of members, headed by Robert Mangaliso Sobukwe, to break away from the ANC. They founded a new group, known as the Pan-Africanist Congress, or PAC.

One of the PAC's first actions was to attack the pass laws. For many black people, the pass they had to carry seemed like a badge of slavery. They were the only ones who had to have passes, and the only ones arrested if they didn't have their passes with them.

The Sharpeville Massacre

The PAC, led by Sobukwe, accused the ANC of not taking action against unjust laws. Sobukwe called on blacks to leave their passes home. He led the way on March 21, 1960. Most people didn't respond to his call. But in Sharpeville, near Johannesburg, Sobukwe's call was answered by fifteen thousand people. The huge crowd gathered at the Sharpeville police station. There, police officers opened fire on the unarmed crowd. Sixty-nine people were killed, and another 180 protestors were wounded.

The massacre brought worldwide attention. Inside South Africa, the people reacted with anger. Mandela and other leaders publicly burned their passes. A strike called by the ANC a week later was the biggest strike ever. Violence erupted, and more people were shot.

The government declared a state of emergency, which meant it could do whatever it wanted. Thousands were arrested, including Mandela and other black leaders. In April, the government

Nelson Mandela burns his pass. Chief Albert Luthuli, president general of the ANC, asked that black people all over South Africa burn their passes as a way of protesting apartheid injustice.

39

Top and above: Most people shot in the Sharpeville Massacre were trying to run away. A huge funeral honored the sixty-nine people killed.

declared the ANC and PAC to be illegal. Rather than disband, however, these organizations decided to continue their work in secret. But many leaders were discouraged. They had tried to change things peacefully and had been ignored, banned, jailed, driven out of the country, and even shot in the process.

In a final attempt at a nonviolent solution, fourteen hundred delegates gathered in March 1961 at what is now called the All-In-Africa Conference. They demanded that the government allow all South Africans to have a part in drafting a new constitution. They also threatened to organize a three-day strike in May if the demand wasn't met.

Nelson Mandela was a surprise speaker at the conference. No one had realized he was no longer under banning orders. He'd been gone so long that some people didn't know who he was. The police swarmed around but weren't able to catch him. He left as soon as he had given his speech.

"We plan to make government impossible. ... I am informed that a warrant for my arrest has been issued and that the police are looking for me. ... [I] will not give myself up to a government I do not recognize."
Nelson Mandela

The Black Pimpernel

After the conference, Mandela returned to the Treason Trial in Pretoria. On March 29, 1961, he and the other accused were freed. Mandela then decided to take his work underground because he believed that he would only be able to continue his work in secret. This way, he might avoid clashes with the police.

After announcing his intentions, Mandela left his home and went into hiding. Moving around the country, he began to get things ready for the three-day strike. Mandela seemed calm and determined to organize the strike himself. In the months that followed, he was nicknamed the "Black Pimpernel," the man the police couldn't catch.

Mandela also managed to stay in touch with the public. He made statements to the press over the phone or through trusted journalists. He traveled around the country dressed in disguises, such as that of a chauffeur or night watchman, that would make him look less like a well-educated lawyer than an ordinary workingman.

"I have had to separate myself from my dear wife and children, from my mother and sisters, to live as an outlaw in my own land. ... I will not leave South Africa, nor will I surrender. The struggle is my life. I will continue fighting for freedom until the end of my days."
Nelson Mandela, describing his life "underground"

41

When the time for the strike finally came, it was only partially successful because the government had done everything in its power to prevent it. Mandela and other leaders began to wonder whether they could continue to preach nonviolence when the government always reacted to the reasonable demands of the people with brute force.

The ANC met secretly with other groups, and they agreed that nonviolence had not worked. They decided to switch to violent resistance. This meeting marked the beginning of a new secret movement, called Umkhonto we Sizwe, or "Spear of the Nation."

Sabotage

Umkhonto we Sizwe struck its first blow by bombing power lines, power plants, and government buildings on December 16, 1961, an Afrikaner holiday. The bombs did not harm any people.

A few weeks after this, Nelson Mandela secretly left the country. He crossed the border into Botswana and traveled across the continent to many African countries. There he met with leaders to seek their help in the fight against apartheid. Officials in African countries like Ghana listened to him and promised their support. Mandela came back to South Africa after a six-month absence, and the police immediately began hunting him again.

"The time comes in the life of any nation when there remains only two choices — submit or fight. That time has now come to South Africa. We shall not submit...."

From a statement issued by Umkhonto we Sizwe, December 16, 1961

Mandela's base was a farm called Lilliesleaf in Rivonia, a suburb outside of Johannesburg. Winnie and their two daughters, Zindzi and Zeni, managed to visit him there, even though the South African police constantly watched them.

Mandela moved around the country in disguise as he built up his organization, often taking the name David Motsamai. But as he was driving away from the city of Durban on August 5, 1962, a police car forced him to pull over. Other police cars quickly followed. Someone had told the police that Mandela would be traveling on that road.

Mandela was charged with inciting black workers to riot and with illegally leaving the country. He was sentenced to five years in prison at Pretoria. After hearing the sentence, Mandela defiantly raised his fist and shouted "Amandla," which means "strength."

Conditions at the Pretoria prison were harsh. Black prisoners were given only a shirt, sandals, and a pair of long shorts to wear. They were given no socks or shoes and had only their shorts to wear in the cold winter weather.

After a few months, Mandela and three other political prisoners were transferred to Cape Town. For the ride there, they were handcuffed to each other inside a truck for all of one night and most of a day. When they arrived at Cape Town, the prisoners were put on a ferry boat bound for Robben Island, a maximum-security prison off the coast of Cape Town.

Trouble at Rivonia

Mandela hadn't been at Robben Island for long when an important event took place. In July of 1963, a van drove up to Lilliesleaf in Rivonia. Police and dogs jumped out, arresting Walter Sisulu and fifteen other people hiding there. The police had tracked down the leaders of Umkhonto we Sizwe.

Winnie Mandela leaves the court during her husband's trial. Nelson Mandela had already been serving a five-year prison term when he was tried and sentenced on other charges. He would not be free to come home to Winnie and their children for twenty-seven years.

After they read some documents found at Lilliesleaf, the police brought Mandela back to Pretoria to face new charges. He was listed as "accused number one." The entire group was charged with organizing bombings and with trying to organize a violent revolution.

In a statement made during the trial, Mandela explained why he and the others had started Umkhonto we Sizwe. He said that the government's policies had made violent resistance by the African people unavoidable. "We felt that without violence there would be no way [for] the African people to succeed in their struggle against the principle of white supremacy. . . . We were placed in a situation in which we had either to accept a permanent state of inferiority, or to defy the government. We chose to defy the law."

Life imprisonment

The Rivonia defendants were found guilty in June 1964. The men could have been sentenced to death because of the seriousness of the crimes. Instead, all of them were sentenced to life in prison.

Mandela and the others in the group who were black or Asian were flown back to Cape Town and taken to Robben Island. This is where Mandela would spend the next eighteen years of his life.

Throughout the 1960s and most of the 1970s, prison conditions were harsh. The

Opposite, above: Nelson Mandela was in prison on Robben Island, seen here from Table Mountain in Cape Town. The prison is surrounded by a rocky coast and icy waters. Opposite, below: Mandela and hundreds of other political prisoners lived under harsh conditions on Robben Island. Here, under the watchful eye of a guard, prisoners break rocks and repair old mailbags in the hot sun.

"More powerful than my fear of the dreadful conditions to which I might be subjected is my hatred for the dreadful conditions to which my people are subjected outside prison throughout this country."
Nelson Mandela

Nelson Mandela's mother, Nosekeni (Fanny), talks to her grandchildren about her imprisoned son.

food was poor, and Mandela and the other prisoners often did not even get the meager food they were supposed to be receiving. Prisoners slept on mats on the concrete floors of their cells. A bucket in each cell served as the toilet. Beginning at 5:30 in the morning, the prisoners had to work long hours in silence. After supper, they had to spend a long night in their cells.

The prisoners were not allowed to listen to radios or to read newspapers. Letters and visits were also restricted: each prisoner was allowed only two letters and two visits a year. To try to improve the situation, Mandela began to use some of the ideas he had put into practice in the freedom movement. Through protest and constant complaint, the prisoners worked to gain improvements on Robben Island. They won better food, warmer clothes, and proper beds. After a while, they were allowed to read newspapers and listen to the radio.

Political prisoners like Mandela urged the other prisoners to demand sports activities and education as a way to keep both their bodies and minds fit. Mandela himself continued to exercise regularly. He also played chess and dominoes and studied enough to finish his law degree.

Winnie's struggle

It was hard for Mandela to be away from Winnie and their children. But the pain of separation was made worse by the way the government was treating Winnie. She was arrested in May of 1969 because of her own political activities and held in jail for seventeen months.

After her release, Winnie was constantly harassed in one way or another. The police raided her home at all hours, and eventually she was banned. She was restricted to Johannesburg and had to ask for permission whenever she wanted to visit Nelson in prison. Because the prison was 950 miles (1,530 km) away, it was a very expensive journey.

Soon she was told to leave Johannesburg and move to Brandfort, 200 miles (320 km) away. Her new home had no electricity, no running water, and no telephone. A public phone booth in the village became her unofficial office, where she went twice a day to make and receive calls.

Black anger explodes

Winnie was being harassed partly because of new black opposition to government policy. An order that black schools should be made to use more Afrikaans triggered a protest known as the Children's Revolt. Twenty thousand schoolchildren marched to protest the order on June 16, 1976. The police began shooting and killed several children. This sparked more opposition, and by the end of the year, hundreds of people, mostly children, had been killed.

"Everyone looked up to him and respected him. When he spoke, we listened. He was patient, tolerant, and I never saw him lose his temper."
Strini Moodley, a prisoner on Robben Island

Winnie Mandela shared her husband's political beliefs and also worked against apartheid. This picture of her was taken in 1965.

Because of forced resettlements and policies regulating workers, many black South African families have been broken up. Only three out of every one hundred black schoolchildren live with both of their parents.

After this, South Africa was never free of protest. More and more people began to remember their jailed leader, Nelson Mandela, and the strength and beliefs of the man on Robben Island.

The government realized that it was hurting itself by keeping him in prison. Throughout the 1970s and 1980s, officials

The Children's Revolt against apartheid erupted on June 16, 1976. It began in Soweto schools but soon spread throughout the country.
Above: This young man was hit by police bullets in the township of Alexandra near Johannesburg.
Left: Clouds of smoke rise from shops and government buildings that were set ablaze during the violence.

In the 1960s, the South African government clamped down on political organizations. But new organizations sprang up as soon as the old ones were declared illegal. In the 1980s, protest groups united in support of ANC goals. At a protest rally, one of thousands of young people wears a Mandela T-shirt.

approached Mandela, telling him they would release him if he promised to leave the country. Each time, Mandela refused. He insisted that once he was a free man, he would do whatever he wanted to do.

Those few people allowed to visit Mandela in prison were impressed by his courage and wisdom. Recognition of Mandela began to spread again. Universities, city councils, and unions around the world began to honor him. Governments and international organizations called repeatedly for his quick release.

To Pollsmoor Prison

Mandela's conditions in prison suddenly changed. In 1982, after eighteen years on Robben Island, he was taken to Pollsmoor Prison, set in a beautiful area near Cape Town. Walter Sisulu and three other Rivonia defendants were also moved.

Mandela's growing reputation was recognized by the government. After having to go to a hospital for an operation, he came back to Pollsmoor to a private cell. The minister of justice began to visit him. Even the guards respected Mandela.

Release — but with conditions

In January of 1985, Pieter Willem ("P.W.") Botha, South Africa's president at that time, offered to free Mandela. The conditions seemed reasonable: Mandela

had to speak out against violence. But Mandela felt that if he did this, he would be speaking out against the struggle of the ANC and the people's fight for freedom.

In response to Botha's offer, Mandela wrote a statement and sent it to his daughter, Zindzi. She read it aloud at a public meeting in Soweto. In the letter, Mandela said he would sit down to discussions with the government only when he and the ANC were free.

The relatively short statement ended with the poweful words, "I cannot and will not give any . . . [support] at a time when I and you, the people, are not free. Your freedom and mine cannot be separated. I will return."

By 1986, people were pressuring South Africa's government to release Mandela and other political prisoners. Armed with only their banners, people often refused police orders to stop demonstrating.

"Nelson Mandela is the power that he is because he is a great man. . . . Our tragedy is that he has not been around to help douse the flames that are destroying our beautiful country."
  Desmond Tutu, Anglican bishop of Johannesburg

Split within the government

The South African government was divided over what to do about Mandela. Some members of the government were afraid of what Mandela would do if he were released. Others argued that they had no choice but to release him.

In 1988, Mandela's seventieth birthday was celebrated all across the world. The highlight of the celebration was a rock concert in London's Wembley Stadium. Over seventy entertainers performed, and 72,000 supporters attended. Millions more watched the concert on live television.

A few weeks after his birthday, news came that Nelson Mandela was ill. Doctors said he had tuberculosis, but he recovered.

On July 11, 1988, a rock concert at London's Wembley Stadium celebrated Nelson Mandela's seventieth birthday. The people attending the concert were only some of the millions of people across the world demanding Mandela's release from prison.

He was placed in a comfortable house at the Victor Verster prison near Cape Town.

By 1989, the country's economy was in trouble. There had been constant strikes and protests, and many countries refused to do business with South Africa because of apartheid. The new president, Frederik Willem ("F. W.") de Klerk, realized that the problems in the economy wouldn't change as long as the working people were not happy. He also knew that to change things he would have to deal with leaders of the ANC and other organizations. And he couldn't deal with them as long as they were in prison.

In October of 1989, de Klerk released eight political prisoners, including Walter

Opposite, above: Nelson Mandela, undefeated by twenty-seven years in prison, speaks to a cheering crowd at a "welcome home" rally in Soweto in 1990.

Opposite, below: The cheering had begun two days before when Mandela went straight from jail to greet his supporters in Cape Town.

"One person has come to embody the aspirations of all of the South African people — Nelson Mandela. His life symbolizes our people's burning desire for freedom; his imprisonment is the imprisonment of the whole South African nation...."

Oliver Tambo,
president of the ANC

Sisulu. On February 2, 1990, he lifted the ban on the ANC and all other groups that had been declared illegal.

Release — at last

Finally, on February 10, 1990, de Klerk announced that he would release Mandela the next day, with no conditions attached.

In his speech to the world on the day of his release, Mandela said his commitment to freedom had not changed: "I wish to quote my own words during my trial in 1964. . . . 'I have fought against white domination, and I have fought against black domination. I have cherished the idea of a democratic and free society in which all persons live in harmony. . . . It is an ideal which I hope to live for and to achieve. But if needs be, it is an ideal for which I am prepared to die.'"

Mandela immediately tried to make his ideal a reality. He met with leaders of the government, and the first formal meetings between the ANC and the government finally took place. A joint working group was set up to deal with the release of prisoners and the return of those who had been forced to leave the country.

Triumph and controversy

As he went to meeting after meeting, Mandela showed that he understood the fears of whites about having an equal society. When he saw how nervous his speeches about sharing the wealth made white business leaders, he made fewer such statements.

Mandela then made a series of trips overseas to Europe, Asia, and North America. Some people were offended when he praised controversial leaders like Yasir Arafat, Fidel Castro, and Muammar al-Qaddafi. But he was only showing them his loyalty, remembering the early days when they had offered their support to the ANC. Nonetheless, he was usually met with praise, including a ticker-tape parade in New York City.

These trips were successful in raising funds for the ANC as it struggled to work out the new policies with the de Klerk government. Mandela also used the trip to convince foreign governments that they should continue restrictions on business with South Africa. Mandela felt that this was one of the best ways to put pressure on the government to end apartheid.

The struggle at home

It was home in South Africa that real effort had to be made. When Mandela was released, many people had unrealistic ideas about what he might be able to achieve. Many South Africans thought his strong personality would be enough to stop the violence that kept springing up between police and black demonstrators, as well as between different black political

groups. These people were disappointed because Mandela couldn't give them exactly what they had expected. Meanwhile, many white groups feared the power he might have, and they threatened even more violence.

In spite of the differing opinions, Nelson Mandela's popularity is still strong among black South Africans. But he has been unable to stop the struggle between the ANC and the Zulu nationalist group, Inkatha. He has also been unable to stop violence between the ANC and other black political groups. Many people imagined Mandela as a superhuman being who could do anything. Yet he is human and has human weaknesses. The real Nelson Mandela is a man of strength and courage who is committed as few others have been to the struggle for freedom.

It is this second Nelson Mandela — Mandela the man — who is doing what he can to end apartheid and resolve one of the world's most unjust situations.

Opposite: Nelson Mandela made a series of visits around the world after his release. In New York, hundreds of thousands of people turned out to welcome him. He was given a traditional ticker-tape parade as his car drove slowly through the streets.

Left: F.W. de Klerk, president of South Africa, is the man who released Mandela from jail. Together, the two men have cautiously begun the task of trying to build a South Africa without apartheid.

To find out more . . .

Organizations

The organizations listed below can provide you with more information about South Africa and apartheid. When you write, be sure to tell them exactly what you would like to know. Always include your full name, address, and age. Also include a self-addressed, stamped envelope.

African National Congress of South Africa (ANC)
P.O. Box 15575
Washington, DC 20003-9997
(Attn: Lindwe Mabuza,
    Chief Representative
    ANC Mission to the United States)

American Committee on Africa
198 Broadway, Suite 402
New York, NY 10038

The Embassy of South Africa
3051 Massachusetts Avenue NW
Washington, DC 20008

Books

The books listed below will help you learn more about Nelson Mandela, South Africa, and apartheid. If you can't find them in your local library or bookstore, ask if they can be ordered for you.

Every Kid's Guide to Understanding Human Rights. Joy Berry
    (Children's Press)
South Africa. Mike Evans (Franklin Watts)
We Live in South Africa. Preben Kristensen and Fiona Cameron
    (Franklin Watts)
Why Are They Weeping? South Africa Under Apartheid. Alan Cowell
    (text) and David C. Turnley (photos) (Stewart, Tabori & Chang)

List of new words

African National Congress (ANC)
An organization made up of different racial groups that was founded in 1912 to work for equal rights for all the people of South Africa.

Afrikaans
A language based on Dutch but including words from other languages. It is spoken by the Afrikaners, the descendants of the first Dutch settlers in South Africa, and by the Coloureds. Attempts to make everyone in South Africa speak and be educated in Afrikaans led to the Soweto riots in 1976.

Afrikaners
Descendants of the first Dutch, French, and German settlers in South Africa, once referred to as Boers. Afrikaners, numbering about 2.2 million, make up about 60 percent of South Africa's white population.

apartheid
An Afrikaans word that means "apart-hood." Apartheid is the official government policy of racial segregation, or keeping people of different races apart, and oppression in South Africa.

Asians
This term is used in South Africa to refer to people whose ancestors came from India.

Bantu
A group of African languages spoken by some seventy million Africans, including almost all black South Africans. Zulu, Xhosa, and Tembu are all dialects of Bantu.

Boers
The original name of the Afrikaners. *Boer* is the Dutch word for farmer.

boycott

A method of nonviolent protest. People boycott whatever they are protesting by refusing to buy or use it.

Coloured

This term is used in South Africa to refer to people with a mixed racial heritage.

de Klerk, Frederik Willem (F.W.) (1936-)

The South African president who, in 1989, vowed to get rid of apartheid and create a more just society in South Africa. De Klerk lifted the ban on the ANC and the PAC and released many political prisoners, including Nelson Mandela.

Gandhi, Mahatma (1869-1948)

An Indian nationalist who led the nonviolent movement that gained independence for India from Great Britain in 1947. His campaign was an inspiration to the ANC and the PAC.

Inkatha

A black nationalist group headed by Chief Gatscha Buthelezi. Its membership is largely Zulu. Since the 1980s, clashes between supporters of Inkatha and the ANC have led to much violence and death.

Pan-Africanist Congress (PAC)

A black South African activist group founded by Robert Sobukwe in 1959. This group felt that the African National Congress (ANC) had become too passive. In general, the PAC has pursued its goals more violently and aggressively than the ANC.

pass laws

A series of laws that restricted black South Africans from traveling outside certain areas. The laws also required black South Africans to carry identification cards at all times. The pass laws were lifted in 1986.

protest
> To speak out against something that people think should be changed; to gather together to oppose a government or a law or policy.

racism
> The idea that one race is better than another. Apartheid is a way of life that is based on racism.

sanctions
> The decision made by one country to refuse to trade with another. Sanctions are often used as a way to put pressure on a country to make changes in its official policies. The United States, Great Britain, and other nations imposed sanctions against South Africa because of apartheid.

segregation
> A policy of separating people, usually by race. Under a policy of segregation, people of different groups cannot marry, attend the same schools, work at the same jobs, use the same transportation, belong to the same churches, shop in the same stores, or eat in the same restaurants.

Soweto
> The South West Township near Johannesburg where almost one million black South Africans live, including the Mandelas.

strike
> To stop working in order to demand better job conditions. People who decide to go on strike usually do so in large groups that want the same changes. This is so that they might have more influence by being unified.

Umkhonto we Sizwe (Spear of the Nation)
> The secret branch of the ANC, organized by Nelson Mandela in 1961, that used terrorist methods to pressure the government to change its policies.

underground

To do something in a hidden or secretive manner. After the Treason Trial ended in 1961, Nelson Mandela decided it was best to work underground.

Important dates

1652 The first permanent settlement is founded at Cape Town.

1835 Over ten thousand Boers leave the Cape and make the Great Trek northeast, where they set up their own independent states.

1899- In the Boer War, the Boers lose their dependent states and
1902 become part of the British colony.

1910 **May 31** — The Union of South Africa is formed from the merger of the British territories and the conquered Boer regions. Blacks are denied the right to vote and any other role in the new government.

1912 **June 8** — The African National Congress (ANC) is founded to unite all black South Africans in the protest against their second-class status.

1918 **July 18** — Nelson Rolihlahla Mandela is born.

1923 New laws establish townships — all-black areas near white towns.

1938 Mandela enrolls at Fort Hare College, where he meets Oliver Tambo.

1941 Mandela and his cousin Justice run away to Johannesburg. There Mandela meets Walter Sisulu, who convinces him to join the ANC.

1942   Mandela enrolls at the University of Witwatersrand to study law.

1943   The ANC Youth League is founded.

1944   Nelson Mandela marries Evelyn Mase.

1948   The racist, pro-Afrikaner National party wins the national election. The policy of apartheid is instituted, and a series of anti-black laws are soon in force.

1949   Marriage between different races is made illegal.

1951   Mandela becomes president of the ANC Youth League.

1952   Chief Albert Luthuli becomes president of the ANC.

1953   Mandela and Oliver Tambo go into partnership as lawyers. In September, Mandela is banned. He is ordered to resign from the ANC and forbidden to attend any meetings.

1955   **June** — The Congress of the People is held in Johannesburg. Delegates approve the Freedom Charter.

1956   **December 5** — Mandela is one of 156 people arrested and charged with high treason. The trial that follows is known as the Treason Trial and lasts four years.

1957   Nelson and Evelyn Mandela divorce.

1958   Nelson Mandela and Winnie Nomzano Madikizela are married.

1959   The Pan-Africanist Congress (PAC) is formed.

1960   **March 21** — The PAC organizes a massive protest against the pass laws. Police open fire on unarmed demonstrators

at Sharpeville, killing 69 people and injuring 180.
March 30 — Mandela arrested, kept in prison five months.
April 8 — The ANC and PAC are banned.
December — Chief Albert Luthuli, president of the ANC, becomes first African to be awarded the Nobel Peace Prize.

1961   Charges are dropped against the last thirty-one defendants in the Treason Trial, including Mandela.

1962   After having traveled through Africa to get support for the ANC, Mandela returns to South Africa. He is arrested and sentenced to five years in jail for leaving the country without a passport and for organizing strikes.

1963   **May** — Mandela is moved to the prison on Robben Island.
July 11 — Police raid Umkhonto we Sizwe headquarters at Rivonia, arrest Walter Sisulu and fifteen others; find proof Mandela founded group and planned many of its activities.
October — Mandela is accused of plotting to violently overthrow the government.

1964   **June 11** — Mandela and the others are found guilty and are sentenced to life in prison.

1973   Mandela is offered release from prison on the condition that he will accept exile in the Transkei region. He refuses.

1976   **June** — The Children's Revolt.

1978   Pieter Willem (P. W.) Botha becomes the new prime minister and vows to get rid of apartheid.

1980   South African hotels, libraries, restaurants desegregated.

1985   Law against marriages between different races is repealed. Botha offers to free Mandela if he will speak out against violence. He refuses.

1986   The pass laws are repealed.
Winnie Mandela forms a private bodyguard, known as the
Mandela Football Club. Over the next several years, the
group is linked to violent activities, including the murder
of a boy, Stompie Moeketsi.

1989   **August** — Frederik Willem ("F.W.") de Klerk replaces
P.W. Botha as head of state.
October 15 — De Klerk releases eight leading political
prisoners, including Walter Sisulu.

1990   **February 2** — De Klerk announces the unbanning of the
ANC, the PAC, and other groups.
February 11 — Nelson Mandela is released from prison.
August — The head of the Mandela Football Club is found
guilty of the murder of Stompie Moeketsi.
The ANC announces that it will cease violent activities
against the government; in return, de Klerk speeds
up reforms.
September — Winnie Mandela is charged with taking part
in the murder of Stompie Moeketsi.
Violence breaks out between the ANC and the Zulu
nationalist group, Inkatha. Hundreds of people are killed.
December — Oliver Tambo, the ANC president who had
been in exile, returns home to South Africa for the first
time in thirty years.

1991   **February** — De Klerk anounces repeal of the Population
Registration Act, Group Areas Act, and various Land Acts.
May — Winnie Mandela is found guilty of kidnapping in
the case of Stompie Moeketsi.

1992   **March** — White South African voters approve move by
de Klerk to share political power and end white minority
rule. De Klerk says the overwhelming vote by more than
2 to 1 has "closed the book" on apartheid and signals the
birth of the new South Africa he promised when elected.

Index

African National Congress (ANC) 4, 12-14, 15, 20, 21, 23, 29, 30, 31, 32, 33, 37-38, 39, 40, 42, 52, 53, 56, 57, 59
AFRICAN PEOPLES: Khoikhoi 6, 7; Pedi 8; Sotho 8; Swazi 8; Tembu 15; Xhosa 8; Zulu 8, 9, 11, 59
Afrikaans 6, 8, 25, 26, 49
Afrikaner National party 25
Afrikaners 6, 7, 42
All-In-Africa Conference 40
ANC Youth League 23, 24, 27, 28
apartheid 6, 24, 26, 28, 29, 30, 32, 38, 39, 42, 49, 51, 55, 57, 59

banning 26, 27, 28, 33, 41
Bantu Education 32
Black Pimpernel 41
Boers 8, 11, 12, 13
Botha, Pieter Willem (P. W.) 52, 53

Chief Jongintaba 17, 18, 19
Children's Revolt 49, 51
CITIES: Cape Town 5, 6, 7, 44, 47, 55; Durban 44; Johannesburg 11, 12, 19, 20, 21, 24, 29, 31, 38, 44, 49, 51; London 54, 55; New York 57, 59; Pretoria 12, 41, 44, 47
Coloured 7, 13, 18, 25

de Klerk, Frederick Willem (F. W.) 55, 56, 59
diamond mines 9, 11

Freedom Charter 33, 34, 35

gold mines 11, 34

Inkatha 59

Luthuli, Albert 39

Mandela, Evelyn Mase 21, 22, 37

Mandela, Henry Gadla 15, 17
Mandela, Nelson Rolihlahla 4; and tuberculosis 55; and Umkhonto we Sizwe 42; arrests of 30, 31, 35, 37, 39, 44; as David Motsamai 44; as general secretary of ANC Youth League 25; as the Black Pimpernel 41; at Pollsmoor Prison 52; at Pretoria Prison 44; at Robben Island 47, 48, 50, 45; at Victor Verster Prison 5, 55; birth and childhood of 15-18; children of 22, 44, 53; divorce of 37; education of 17-19, 21, 22, 48; establishes law practice 29; forms the ANC Youth League 23; goes underground 33, 41; joins ANC 23; marriages of 21, 37; release from prison 56; trials of 31, 37, 41, 44, 47
Mandela, Nosekeni (Fanny) 16, 17, 48
Mandela, Winifred "Winnie" Nomzamo Madikizela, 4, 37, 38, 44, 48-49

Pan-Africanist Congress (PAC) 38, 39, 40
pass laws 14
Population Registration Act 25

segregation 11, 14, 18, 23, 26
Sharpeville Massacre 39, 40
Sisulu, Walter 21, 23, 37, 45, 52, 56
Sobukwe, Robert Mangaliso 38, 39

Tambo, Oliver 28, 29, 37
TOWNSHIPS: 14, 19, 20, 22, 23, 30; Alexandra 19, 21, 51; Sharpeville 39-40; Sophiatown 19; Soweto 51, 53, 56
Treason Trial 37, 41

Umkhonto we Sizwe 42, 45, 47
Union of South Africa 13